# sharp
# blue
# stream

poems

# david lawton

THREE ROOMS PRESS

NEW YORK CITY

*Acknowledgements*

*Unfurl* appeared in the *Brownstone Poets Anthology* (2012)

*While Listening* appears in *Venetian Hour: Dinner with the Muse Part II* (2013)

*Sonny Rollins* appeared in *Erato* (Feb./March, 2007)

*Vision South of Rivington* and *Yorkville* appear in *Slices of the Apple* (Spiny Babbler, 2013)

*Strip Mall in the Poconos* and *Between a Brother and Sister* appeared in *The Best of Stain, Volume 2* (2009)

*Tri-City Rock Brood* appeared in *It's Animal but Merciful* (greatweatherforMEDIA, October 2012)

*Buk Drops In* appeared in *Polarity eMagazine* (Fall 2011)

*Chanticleer* appeared in *hell strung and crooked* (Uphook Press, 2010)

*The 31st of May* appeared on *http://octoberbabies.wordpress.com/*.

*Sharp Blue Stream*

Editor:
Peter Carlaftes

Cover and Interior Design:
KG Design International, New York, NY (katgeorges.com)

Front Cover Art:
"Zouk Stream" by Russ Johnson (russjohnsonart.blogspot.com)

Back Cover and Page 98 photo:
Jodi Lynn Concepcion (shutterunderground.com)

First Edition
ISBN: 978-0-9884008-6-3

Published by
Three Rooms Press, New York, NY
threeroomspress.com

*This book is dedicated to the memory of
James F. Lawton, Jr. (1931–1993)
and Virginia Lawton Duffett (1955–2009),
who believed in me without question.*

## Confessional

I have a secret to tell you,
Cutting very close to the bone:
I don't know if I'm going to make it anymore.

And I have another secret,
Close to the surface of the skin:
I love my failures and I'd welcome many more.

# contents

sharp
blue
stream

## Into the Dark Mysterious

When I come to you in the night
Into the dark mysterious
I move to the rhythm of your steady bedded breath,
Sturdy within its pillow-softness

And teeter on the edge,
Trying to be accepted by your ripeness
You hot tropical wildflower
Tightly closed in morning night.

You answer my touch with a sound of recognition
A musical note.
A thrum. A chime.

You are happy faraway in your dreams,
But your body knows me.
From faraway, you recognize me.
You welcome me.

You open yourself to me
And you give me your mouth
Cool wellspring quenching
And unquenching me.

I lie there dumb with happiness
In the thoughtless stillness night
And happiness lasts forever
Because you never forget the moments
you were happy

## Drink

He stands in the floodlight of the Frigidaire
With his pillow-soft paunch,
And he scratches himself unconsciously;
His blue eyes beady behind thick prescriptions
As they slather over fatteners that he is forbidden.

He'd sneak a peek at the cheesecake quick
Or scoop some chink-food
From cardboard into his yawning cavern;
But those God blessed damn kids would turn him in,
Yak to his betty how he's breaking his diet.

His world is his responsibilities
And always has been and it exhausts him.
He does not look beyond his own backyard;
He believes we are going to a better place;
He drinks the milk straight out of the carton.

And the cry goes up:

> *"Drinking out of the bottle,*
> *Drinking out of the bottle."*

The cry one as old as his oldest children,
Who learned it from rote from his betty and used it
To turn in their father, make points with their mother,
Catching him in the light of the Frigidaire.

They learned from their Dad how to drink from the carton;
How to let all the cold air run out of the box;
Now it's his turn to singsong the cry through the household,
Spinning 'round like a dervish, a low comedy clown.

*"Drinking out of the bottle,*
*Drinking out of the bottle."*

How did you do it? How raise seven children?
How go to the office and bring office home?
How believe politicians? How believe in salvation?
How you did not go crazy's what I want to know.
He tilts his head back and he opens his throat;
His Adam's apple keeps time with a crystalline sound;
He stands solidly sway-backed,
And he dribbles some on him.

And the cry goes up:

*"Drink!"*

## Positively Gothic

After another endless night where I relieved the stress and frustration of trying to endure in the city and possibly find some truth by abusing my body with drugs and wine, in manic desperate company, I step out into a hushed world, the air rich with stillness, my path homeward a dark column of buildings, positively gothic.

A constellation of fat stars of snow make the long slow fall out of the deep black skies of New York, like ball bearings in motor oil (America, you taught me how to think this way and ruin a perfectly good poem. Your T.V. ads showed me how).

Short Edwardian buildings whisper their pasts, when their storefronts had dignity. Ancient grey gargoyles coo their pigeons to sleep. Tall marble obelisks wink out their lights as they exhaust their use, as if striking electric bell chimes.

A sixties condo building, like a high-tech Aztec temple, extends itself upward toward the heavens in suspended meditation.

And the Flatiron, the empirical wonder of New York – industrial freak.

An American flag displayed overhead fills me with conflicting emotions: of how we have misused her; of how she whip-cracks smartly in a gust of wind. My eyes are filled with tears at the holy sweet silence, the ceasefire called on the battlefield, overcome with the joy and excitement of my life at this moment.

Then it's the Met Life clock tower, always five minutes fast. Gets us all on the run again.

## When The Chelsea Was The Chelsea

You'd enter through a lobby
Like a funhouse mirror
Can you tell the famous art
From the amateur slop?

Then the elevator'd take you
To a hallway skanky with skunk
Blended subtly with cat pee
Bouquet strangely reassuring

Right through chaotic doorway
To wild-eyed hipsters goading nihilistic cynics
Euroart cartoons amuse scruffy student angels
And not nearly enough women
Ever present in the moment
All together stewing in the pot

The stereo would play you
Ornette Coleman or Coleman Hawkins
The Fifth Dimension and the MC5
All of them turned up too high

So as I push my way through
I hear goatee stroking dude ask,
"Who you talkin' 'bout, Big Joe Turner?!"
And soul patch puller replies,
"No, Peter Kropotkin!"

In the corner,
Wreathed in a cloud of reefer,
Attended by a crowd of
Ice blue German tourists:
Huncke, like an opiated yogi –
Heavy-lidded, wizened,
His third eye aflutter
Stretching his neck like a turtle
He draws himself up
And us in to confide:

"A pointy dick.
I always wanted one.
Like a dog's dick."

## Herbert

Inspiration to the Beat
Patron saint of the street
Turned Burroughs onto smack
Once did the nasty with Jack

Huncke the Junky!

I'd've described him as elfin
But he'd've bitch-slapped me silly
He was the consummate hustler
But he counseled me to be more trusting
Europeans lined up to kiss his ass
While he said he was "no big deal"

Huncke the Junky!

He did whatever shit he wanted until the end
I couldn't have been prouder to call him my friend
Street people showed their respect when he walked around the city
He owes me sixty dollars for the rest of eternity.

Huncke the Junky!

## A Ghost Story

I had a friend in kindergarten
I called him Spooky
Because he liked ghosts and ghouls,
Zombies and monsters. And I went
Over to his house and watched
*Bewitched* with him on TV.
Flickering images in silver and grey,
Like tapering gradations of ash.

And at recess we played "chase the girls"
And we would make the girls scream
A bloodcurdling scream.
That was me and Spooky.

Then we didn't go to school together for quite a few years.
When we did, it was like we played for different sides.
He looked like a burn-out in his leather biker jacket,
Long bangs shrouding heavy metal eyes.
I was a certified band nerd, but when we saw each other
In the hall, a secret grin passed between us. The
Phantom presence of our childhood. BOO!

I heard he joined the Air Force
Supposed to be his wild blue yonder
Where they sent him to broadcast school
So he developed skills for the TV job pool

That's how he came to be in Tower #1
On that brilliant Indian Summer morning;
Watching Channel 2's antenna on the 110th floor,
Never dreamed there was a holocaust aborning.

And it's not my fault
I didn't know you were in New York
But I couldn't have saved you anyway
I was all the way uptown.

I think of you high in the stratosphere
So close to heaven with no place else to go
And I don't know
I didn't really know you
I don't want to know what you went through

And I didn't do nothing
I tried to give blood.

Did you get a last moment?
How does one say goodbye?
Did your life pass before you?
What did it all add up to?

That night, my mother-in-law called
My wife and I and said,
"We'll drive up and get you."

But we couldn't save you
So we wouldn't leave you.
We stayed here to breathe you,
When the wind blew uptown.
Now my cells have absorbed you
And my memory's restored you
You cannot be forgotten
Because you're in my blood.

Spooky, old friend, you'll forever haunt me
With a childish grin that made the little girls scream.
All the spirits in white sheets and rubber masks
Bow their heads as your shadow does pass.

We never knew
We'd ever know
Real horror.

*(In memory of Robert E. Pattison 1960-2001)*

## Unfurl

Little dude
Alone
At play in the park
Lend me your Batman cape

I'm running away
In the nick of time
And I haven't a minute to spare

I want to unfurl
Signal single repair
Laying out angst
In my serrated trail
In the sometimes marshmallow wind

Zowie! Ka-Powie!
Wham Bam Ka-Boom!
Brought to you in
Living Colorform hues
A cartoon Super Saturday
Bazooka bubble pop
Squeaky magic marker
Wrings ecstatic funky chicken
Check my grape juice mustache
Darling mother, never leave me

Duh-nuh nah nah
Nah nah nah nah
Doo wah diddy
You bet your sweet bippy
Dig the barefoot hippie
Eat a bowl of crispy bwiti!

Playing paradiddles
With pixie sticks
Licorice whips
Lik-m-aid and
Nik-l-nips

Articulated clockwork robot
Smugly blowing rubber bladders
Bristling ozone burst of
Kirby cosmic energy
Explodes molded plastic gears
Launched slinky springs
Boing oing oing oing

I must away
To my secret hideout
Lock the door
To your hidden compartment

Same bat time and
Same bat channel
Reminds of the glide
That can set you free

You have the power
To make bad shit cower
When they see you
Run away into the breeze.

## Answering the Bell

The day is fin'lly dimming
Us kids are still out playing
A distant bell starts ringing
The ice cream man is coming

My army has been winning
This game of war exciting
Attention now is waning
The ice cream man is coming

Cherry Bomb, Jimmy Cone, Rocket Pop
White Rock Cola naked lady can
Toasted Almond, Choc-O-Malt, Italian Ice
He says tomorrow he will come again

My sticky spoon's attracting
Mosquitoes endless buzzing
The bell grad'ally fading
The ice cream man departing

I wonder where he's going
And if his job's fulfilling
If someone's at home waiting
For the ice cream man returning

Summer replacement TV show
Is beginning its lonely run
I recognize that black guy from something else
Now what's his name again?

I lie here widely wond'ring
New school year's approaching
While we all are wint'ring
Where's the ice cream man going?

## Salisbury Beach Clown

In Shaheen's Fun-o-Rama Park
At the Salisbury Beach Amusement Park
There was a giant clown
Sitting on the roof
He must have been twenty feet tall
Painted all white
With dots of color here and there
He would've been a lame looking clown
Except for his mad height
Which really creeped me out
His clowny legs straddled
The rolling barrel entranceway
Of the slapstick vintage funhouse
With its teetering staircases
Shape changing mirrors and
Shocking blast of air
Up between your legs
This clown loomed large
Through the dark ride of many a nightmare
Without a jumbo dunk tank
Big enough to hold him
Yet I longed to see him
Basking in the sunshine
With the coming of each spring
But some humorless arsonist
Made quick work of my clown
Real estate being more profitable than fun
He cleared the way for more shitty condos
White trash could default on
And once again I am left
With this sorrowful parting
This broken carnival music
That made Del Shannon run away
All I need is

To smell the greasy onion rings
And I am
The fat boy at the end of the booth
Watching the cool kids burst my balloon
Soft serve dribbling jimmies
Down the sides of my Tast-I-Kone
While I try to work up the courage
To ride the Roundabout
That clown sits mounted
In the back of my mind
Like he's riding
The ghosts of the flying horses
And his mocking laughter
Sounds distinctively
Like a rusted steam calliope.

## Solstice

On the corner of Harvard and Comm
In Allston
What we called the student ghetto
Of Boston
I met my green-eyed Jewess enchantress
On a day in summer
When we both still were young

Adorable and adoring
Reflecting cloud movements
In lime chiffon
Her lips curled up at a mischievous angle
And musical words merged
With her quicksilver tongue:

"Your red highlights sure sparkle
When you're out in the sun."

Many years flown since this encounter
We were in love,
But I found reason to doubt her
We married others
After drifting apart
Experience earned us each a
Healthy heavy heart

But to this very day,
When in summer
Young women cast a spell
With sparkling words and eyes
I refuse to cover my head from the swelter
Lest last red highlights
Lose occasion to thrive.

## The Departed

*I: Dorothy, the Old German Lady Downstairs*

Now you are gone, gone forever.
Gone from the plastic yogurt containers
You hoarded to drink beer out of;
Gone from your spot on the stoop where you
Waited for the UPS to bring the shipments
Of cigarettes that would kill you.
From your cuckoo clock and your Hummel figurines;
Your thick black eyebrow pencil and your
Groaning shopping cart.

Still the building breathes you out:
Your tobacco smoke and your boiled dinner;
Your paranoia about FDR and Churchill
Ruining the Reich; your prejudice towards
Any vaguely dark-skinned person you did not know.
All slowly dissipating, like your lonely funeral train.

*II: My Wife, Mrs. Lawton*

Now you are gone, gone from my life.
Gone to find yourself by leaving me behind;
Leaving behind your things for only so long.
Not so long ago we bought a linen chest of wood,
Vaguely Victorian. A piece for our future
Where we could keep our nice things. Sometimes
At night I open it and stand there and remember
All that was precious.

Breathe deep, breathe it in:
Scented candles and French milled soap;
Cucumber lotion, and freshly laundered sheets
Folded just so. A woman's touch, a girlish way
About her; comfort and care and companionship.
Soon these words I write will be the only way left
To recall my highest aspiration.

## Vision South of Rivington

What just happened?
I was turning the corner
And what caught my eye?
Serious mysterious woman
Gave me special secret smile.
Me. Millions of people here
But that smile was just for me.
Why special smile for me?
Was it my after shave? My shoes?
Tell me how to replicate
Disintegration of the blues.
What did she see? Did she see
The real me? Can she ask him to call?
His absence caused a general pall.
Doesn't she know I'm not the man
I had been? Can I even be sure
Of what I'd just seen?

Check it:

Downtown boho beauty conveyed
Mystic cryptic knowledge with her
Optic twinkle and her flower-sniffer's crinkle
And a sun spot beaming off her
Gold nose ring. Snap! Nose rings are
The only things from this day forth!
Then blithely, lithely walk away
Tossing gossamer over a shoulder,
Veiling enigmatic static in a
Cool Pashmina breeze.

The feeling I have is total.
Close to combustibility.
Explode a load of mighty soul,
Ejaculate my jocularity!
Her smile did not laugh at me
But giggled alongside.
That we cannot remain simple, pure.
That passion can't abide.
An everyday miracle. An infusion of life.
A restoration of the faith. Nose ring sunbeams
Strafing strife.

Sometimes people recognize each other
When they are never going to meet.
Maybe sometimes a moment
Is all that all can be.

## To a Young Poetess

*(for CW)*

Keep on turning
Spinning, whirling
Stirring the microbes
As you move through space

All the while,
The gears conforming
And words are forming
An organic line
Like a creeping vine
In the mossy gardens
Of your emerald mind

Don't let them tell you
What it is
Or who you are
For you can go far
But, daughter, never so far
As you've already been
Inside.

Spiral onward
Gyroscoping
Beveling, sloping
Around every bend
Your instincts always spotting for you
Balancing truth and beauty
As you corkscrew through

Tell us what it is
And who you are
And who you ain't
Your words are paint
And your heart's on fire
Illustrate and illuminate
How the pirouette turns you
Inside.

## While Listening

I was listening to something or other
But I was gazing at her placid naked ankle
Elegantly languid,
Crossed over a thigh;

Long silky fingers,
With nails buffed to a luminescent sheen
Traced a line along the top of her expensive pump
Against her skin, all peaches and cream;

Back and forth her dewy digit
Seemed to probe for an enveloping home
I started to fantasize that I could be
A shoe horn of my vision's very own;

And all the while she remained poised
As she seemed to listen to what I cannot say
With sublime profile and a serene smile
Her satin fingers wiped all the words away.

## Sonny Rollins

He doth bestride these narrowing times like a colossus;
The last of a race of giants.
The essence of excellence. Virtuosity embodied
In a shambling, grandfatherly grizzly bear.
An eager audience of greater New York jazz cats
Braved ominous forecasts to dig Sonny out of doors.

A dependable groove straight out of pocket switched us on,
Swinging with authority and a touch of Latin flavor,
Like a pinch of musical adobo. Then THE SOUND,
A greasy fat growl, like pork and beans with hot sauce.
A rolling roiling rumbling thunder from a steam engine
Made of brass. I was tapping the six-eight and swaying
Like a rabbi at the wailing wall. He was delivering
The show we all expected at seventy-plus.

When he said that was it for the night, the true believers
Shouted back as one, "Don't Stop This Carnival!"
And as the tourists headed out into the evening,
He leaned in toward us conspiratorially and
Let his axe rip up the night sky, tearing the fabric
Of the moment, the keys firing like pistons.

The whole Manhattan skyline seemed to bow down
And listen, as my poor sad soul began to rise.
All the possibilities – in a song, in a life – lifting me up.
That harmonic convergence they speak of.
The Williamsburg Bridge was so proud that all that
Woodshedding paid off.  Addiction and complacency
Be damned. Redemption is possible! (I'm sorry I doubted you, Jesus)

Finally the great man stepped to the mic and croaked,
"Don't forget . . . to don't forget".
What won't I ever forget?
In the end, genius stands alone.

## Wisdom

In the midnight hour
I return once again
To my intimate friend
The tide is wise

Ever playing variations
On its constancy
All which wear away
Distraction's inner noise

The moon its magic lantern
Drenched with juicy silver light
Casting a thousand flecks of moonshine
On the pulsing sea

Mellow woodsmoke in the night
Scent of sweetly salted pine
Each do their part to unwind;
Enshrouding, cleansing fog
Richly caressing ocean breeze
Each have the power to please.

Under a patchwork sky of clouds
Or a clear celestial dome
An elemental, essential calm
Enters the center of my being

I know I am alone
Alone with everybody else
On the only planet that we have
Teach me how to ebb and flow

The tide is wise.

## Body Surfing in New Hampshire

First thing is
Most times
You must brave some icy water
Painfully brisk
You'll want to scuttle away
Like the sandpiper on the shore
But don't go
Gut it out
Hop from frozen stump to stump
As you inch your way deeper
Arms drawn up
Like a boxing kangaroo
Face tense
Why didn't I just dive in?
I just couldn't
I must ease
My most vulnerable area in gingerly
Have courage
Get out a little farther and
A wave will baptize your private parts
And then
What the hell
You jump in
And when you pop back up
You are Aquaman
Or Prince Namor, the Sub-Mariner
Triumphant
Hey! This water's not that cold
Damn! I feel like a kid again
I don't want the summer to end!

Next thing is
You must practice patience
Bobbing in the water
Like the marker for a lobster trap
Reading the waves

Eyeing the curl
Anticipating the break
Timing is everything
Ducking under the ones
That don't serve your purpose
Or would cartwheel you
Through your wipeout
Or taking the hit
Letting it slap across your back
Exploding spray
And then the moment arrives
Turned sideways you recognize
That the wave will meet you
You turn and dive
A human torpedo
I become part of the wave
Enveloped in buoyancy
Hurtling through churning foam
'Til I am crawling on my belly
At the shoreline
Like my ancient ancestors
Emerging from the ooze
Exultant, I bound back in
As a middle aged dad
Leaves his kids on the beach
To become a kid himself again
Peripherally matching up with me
And the breaker
And it's on
The momentary submersion
In the opalescent briny
An escape from the surface world
I come in with the tide
Outpacing the suburban dad
Only to scamper back in
To the bright rich water

Like an ocean naiad
Over and over again
Wicked pissa!
I don't want this moment to end!!!
I carry this joy off the beach with me
And walk home
Dripping euphoric swagger.

## Issue of Intimacy

Another experiment in online dating
Another neighborhood in Brooklyn
More getting-to-know-each-other conversation
More red wine means a chance I might get in.

She asked me back to her place
That's progress for me on a first date
There was tequila and ganja for dessert
Then she laid herself out on a plate

But when I looked up from my efforts
I found a sight that was strangely funny
My hooded sweatshirt was twisted all around her head
Like the wrappings of an Egyptian mummy

She removed her head
And that erased me
And left behind only
Her naked ass and pussy

An open invitation to sexual assault
No engagement. No commitment.
No involvement. No one's fault.

But that lovely ivory body
Lying so cold and still
Was enough to make a satyr pause
And cause his fiery loins to chill

It looked to be the work of the master
Monsieur Auguste Rodin
And I don't jack off in museums
Unless the exhibit puts its hand down my pants.

## Frequency

*Beep. . .Beep. . .Beep. . .Beep.*

Radio Tower, Radio Tower
What do you send?
And where does it end?
Radio Tower, Out my back window
Off in the distance
Past the cattails
Radio Tower, Steel girder giant
On the horizon
Eye blinking red
You make me ponder
What's out there yonder
Where your transmission clears
The stratosphere
What tropical atoll
Receives your signal?
Your waves radiate tow'rd
The city tonight
Radio Tower, Hour after hour
I wait here contemplating
Your frequency
You have all the power
Pick me up now, or
Bounce me through space
Between your satellites
Radio Tower, Please take me farther
Away from this nowhere
On your tracking beam
Transmit my wonder
Like lightening from thunder
An endlessly arcing invisible pulse

*Beat. . . Beat. . . Beat. . . Beat.*

## American Invocation

All hail the American garage!
The oil spot slick stage
Whiff of go-go gasoline
Built-in reverb echo chamber
The trash can crash
Frosted flake crunch
Scratching on the bed springs
Of your brother's top bunk

All hail the followers of
Chet Atkins and Duane Eddy
From Ron Asheton to Jack White
For the jangle and the twang
The fuzz and the squeal
The relentless drive of a hammered line
Through flailing waves of ringing chords

All hail the drummer
Working the backbeat and fills
His shaggy hair in contrapuntal motion
To his steady bass drum pedal

All hail the keyboardist
Of the Hammond and the Vox
Bringing the sounds of church and carnival
Sliding and colliding together

All hail the bass guitarist
Rock steady standing stock still
Thumpin' and bumpin' the beat
Without ever losing their cool

And all hail the front man

Mumbling like a bluesy method actor
Screaming and shouting himself hoarse
His feet possessed with the boogaloo
His hips getting fresh with the tambourine

Whether decked out in funky Minuteman garb
Or sporting a turban and velvet robe
In matching suits or leathers or Martian sunglasses
Nehru jackets or paisley or daishikis

All hail The Kingsmen slurring *Louie, Louie*
The Electric Prunes having *Too Much to Dream Last Night*
Hail Skye Saxon and The Seeds *Pushin' Too Hard*
And the UK's Troggs laying down *Wild Thing*

Hail The Remains of Boston
Opening the final tour of The Beatles
The MC5 kickin' the jams
In the bloody streets of Chicago
Hail The Stooges raw power
In a studded dog collar
Playing on the radios in Queens listened to
By the future Ramones

They made us hear the interstate highway cruise
The hot rod ripping up the lonely road
The frat boys frenzied anarchy
The surf culture sunsplashed endlessly

All hail!
Hail!
Hail!
Rock and roll.

## Alberta and Ruth

Alberta fled Memphis for Chi-town
At the tender age of twelve
She couldn't wait to sing that good time music.
Entertaining pimps and criminals at Dago Frank's
Helped pay her mama's fare north
What kept mom from going back
Were gigs at the Panama, the Elite, and the DeLuxe Café
Until Miss Hunter became the "Sweetheart of Dreamland".
Writing songs of Handy Men and Ramblin' Gals
Always living life her own way
She gave Bessie Smith the *Downhearted Blues*
Became the toast of Paris in the 1930s
Starred for the USO in the WWII.
But her mama got sick and died
And she thought the business had passed her by
So she took a nursing course at the age of 59.
She said twenty years working in a New York hospital
Taught her the priceless value of being kind.
But Goldwater Memorial decided to retire her
Because they thought she was 61
They never dreamed she was twenty years older!
Whatever her age, she was bored sitting at home
And that good time music called to her again.
Soon she was cookin' at The Cookery
Her butterfly mobile earrings swinging
As she strutted in her bordello fringed curtain shawl
Like a vision from The Dreamland Café.
All ages wondered at her ageless vitality
Her castle kept rockin' until she was 89.

Ruth ran away with a trumpet player
When she was only seventeen
She got fired from singing with Lucky Millinder
Because she brought the band drinks for free.
But there was something about the way she sang a torch song
That made them call her the girl with the teardrop in her voice

And there was something about the way she rocked the beat
That had the cats and chicks calling her Little Miss Rhythm.
Sixteen top tens and five number ones
Made Atlantic Records "The House That Ruth Built"
*So Long, Teardrops from My Eyes* and
*(Mama) He Treats Your Daughter Mean*
made R&B stand for RUTH and BROWN.

But shit happens in this life
That takes you out of the limelight
Miss Brown found herself single parenting two sons
Clerking in stores and scrubbing white people's floors
Simply to keep them all together.
But some people hadn't forgotten her
And she wasn't about to forget how to sing
There was Motormouth Maybelle in *Hairspray*
And a Tony for *Black and Blue*
And a Grammy for her comeback album too
And Ruth spoke out for her fellow pioneers
The architects of rock and roll
"We just want what we earned,"
was the Foundation of her call.
Now this little girl's gone rockin'
I hope she has a good time
And tells Mister Fitzgerald in heaven
That he couldn't always tell reason from rhyme
There *are* second acts in American life
Something Alberta and Ruth both knew about
Another is it's a good day for the blues
When you can sing the blues out.

## For My Sister

Oh my sister
You sat my diapered bum on your lap
Like a China doll
You held my hand when we crossed the street
You took me to the Herman's Hermits movie
At the old Strand Theatre
I told you jokes and stories
You made me put on a show
How can I thank you?
Why would I blame you?

You included me with your older friends
You helped me through skin care disasters
I stared out the window from the top bunk
When you came home from dates
You helped me buy a friendship ring
I sang for you at your wedding
What did we know?
How could we know?

Oh my sister
I couldn't be where I am today without you
And look what we have come to
With no place left to run to
When you look in the mirror, it's hard to bear
The disappointment, the grabbing fingers
The prying eyes, the lies, so many calling 'round
With nothing to bring to the table

What can we do about the acts of others?
How did our parents teach us
What was right to do?
It doesn't matter
Just because it matters
When I look in the mirror, it's hard to bear

The uncertainty. Never knowing why.
The failure. The weakness.
The awkward moments by and by.

Even if you can see it,
Like an old picture on the wall
I can't be there
But it wouldn't make a difference
If I was there.
What could be different here or there?

What can we say on a Saturday night
With a straight face
In two different cities
Over a telephone line?:

You are wonderful.
You are better than all this.
I am your sympathetic shadow

## Flight

I need someone to hold onto me
Or I might fly away.
I'm an angel, you see. . .
. . . or so I have been told.

An angel. An angel. Covered in light.
Impossibly good. Impossibly white.
I know that the poet says,
"Every man is an angel",
But how me when I am too much the fool?

To dwell in Elysium,
To breathe pure bliss.
Covered with glory eternal.
Messenger divine.
Quicksilver intermediary.
Guardian. Protector.
Bringer of perpetual assistance.
Entering in with an open heart,
My breastplate hung loose at my side.

I am here. I am near for you.
I still care. Trust I'm there for you.

Solitary sentinel. Loving and alone.
Laughing at myself. Next time, thrust it home!
Serving the host of heaven. One going. One sent.
For staying is nowhere. And flight my ascent.
Edifying in my rightness, the grievous angel sighs
From the cockpit of my aerie,
A moral high ground in the sky.

Hopeless. Waiting. The cold gath'ring 'round me.
I give myself so fully. How e'er can I hold back?
I know that the poet says,

"Every angel is terrifying",
But how can I when I am so afraid?

A clarion call from the ether shrieks
Of vengeful rebels with black wings.
Furious Moloch and his dark brothers
Rise defying our hierarchies.
The sky crackles as blazing swords
Forge a smelted empyrean firmament.
We are the champions of the moment of truth
But this moment (in truth) too shall pass.

I cannot bear the burden
Of the alabaster feathers.
No more jewels for my crown
In heaven. **LET ME FALL!**

A blue angel
Tumbling through azure sky,
The rapture so ecstatic
With celestial evanescence.
Beyond the veil, the wind
Whipping and hurtling
One sullied, solid
Organic being earthward.

I need someone to hold onto me
Or I might fly away.
Fly from flying. From me.

## P.S. from my Estranged Wife

"If there is old flour in the cupboard, throw it out."

What was that?

"If there is old flour in the cupboard, throw it out."

A year and a half from the time she walks out on me,
That's her afterthought?

Poor old flour. Whatever did you do to be the
One thing that could've gotten into her craw
And make her turn back. I hope you make it gnaw!
I'm jealous of you, flour. I'm almost mad at you.
But I cannot do you in, for I'm becoming old too.
If I dump you in the trash, I'm no better than her.
To give up on you is a kind of murder.
If I throw you out, where does it end?
Where do I begin? What kind of message does it send?
Should I get rid of everything that she ever touched?
Twelve years of history shouldn't mean that much?
Maybe I should just firebomb this place.
Incinerate it clean. Do not leave a single trace.
I'll tell you why not. I don't want to be too alone.
A flour can make a man smile. Can't you throw a dog a bone?
I'm sure she was afraid that the flour would attract bugs
Who would root down in it as if finding mom's dugs.
How they'd get inside the zip-lock is a separate mystery.
A spontaneous generation of some kind of cooties.
Hey – maybe they'll bake me cookies like she sometimes used to do.
Beggars can't be choosers. You gotta take what's offered you.
That flour's Enriched, Unbleached, All-Purpose.
These bugs might grow like they're on 'roids.
To analyze where this is going might take a gross of Sigmund Freuds.
When these mutant weevils bust out of the cupboard,
They smell distinctly of female musk.
I will readily submit myself to their ravishment
If they promise to properly dispose of my husk.

## Satisfaction

My sainted Irish Catholic mother
Refrains from smoke and drink
Hardly ever leaves the house
She's as quiet as a mouse

My mother has no past
But marriage to my dad
All-around upkeep of our brood
Gen'ral example of moral rectitude

But there's this one thing
About my mother
That just doesn't seem
To jibe

My mom loves Mick Jagger
Though she doesn't care about the Stones
My mom loves Mick Jagger
Though she's never even rock and rolled

It's something 'bout the way his body moves
It's like rubber on a hot August day
Even when she wants to turn the volume down
She has to watch him when his hips start to sway

And even though she still prefers the song delivery
Of a white bread crooner like the late Dick Haymes
When Mick smirks at the camera like the naughty boy he is
My mom is forced to relinquish former claims

My prim and proper suburban mother
May seem an unlikely Jagger fan
But she feels like there is no crime
Enjoying a fellow senior citizen having such a damn good time

## Everything I Need to Know

Whenever I feel no one understands me
That I am too weird or distant
To connect with anyone at all

I think of Van Morrison
In his rhinestone pajamas
Onstage in *The Last Waltz*

Such a beautiful mess
A schlumpy ecstatic
Uncomfortably lone

And in that moment
I think maybe
I might get by.

## Irish Up

Don't ever piss off an Irishman
Because Irishmen are totally mad
They run into blazing infernos
Take frigid dips New Years Day barely clad

Don't ever tee off a bog trotter
For you will drive the man out of his mind
He'll go charging lion-hearted through the gates of Hell
Haven't you heard of the Fighting 69th?

Remember the hitch in Cagney's shoulders?
Tommy gun time step rat-a-tat-tat
The brutality of a sneer
That instilled all with fear
And preceded Jimmy knocking someone flat.

Don't you ever tick
                    off a sod who's a mick
Bobby Sands measured grit by the pound
Though they may destroy themselves in proving their point
They will do their best to also bring you down.

## Ripley's Yule Log

He made us a Christmas mix tape
He was a member of the same gym as we
He was much closer to my wife than me
I'm not sure if I can recall his name:

Marvin? Melvin? Norman? Carlton?

He was a gay dude with a very gentle way
An infectious smile that would brighten your day
And a terminal case of full-blown AIDS
Like so many friends I had known before:

John and Jim. Another John. New Age Otis. Joyboy Joe.

His tape had campy clips of Joan Crawford and Divine
Mister Greenjeans sang to Captain Kangaroo
Liberace played *O Tannenbaum* and *We Wish You a Merry Christmas* too
And many more that made the Yuletide fabulous:

Brenda Lee. Mae West. Ella. ABBA. Connie Francis.
Patty and Maxene and LaVerne.

My wife left the tape behind along with me
Hell, now cassettes are totally out of date
It was years ago he met his fate
I don't think I'll ever remember his name.

But he hardly even knew us
And he never stopped smiling
Even while he was dying
He was sharing things I never heard before

I will keep this shit when the wheels have stopped turning
Because I want to remember every good thing
Like I want you to remember when I told you
He made us a Christmas mix tape.

## Boy of the Year

Charlie McMahon was Boy of the Year
Let's hear it for Charlie! Charlie McMahon!
Boy of the Year in my hometown, in 1971.

A typical kid from the suburbs
Pop gun and tree fort and paper route
A blessing upon his mother's heart
And a pride for his father as well

Charlie hung out at the Boy's Club
Swimming and diving and practical jokes
He worked with kids as he got older
A natural leader was Charlie McMahon

His senior year he won a trophy, named
For the first kid from Woburn killed in Vietnam
The club's director told his Marine's stories
Inspiring curiosity in Charlie McMahon

Charlie trained hard to be an Embassy guard
And wouldn't you know that he made the grade
He came home proudly in his new dress uniform
Before he shipped out for the fall of Saigon

The other Charlie didn't give a shit
They were sick and tired of colonial powers
We forgot how pissed off people can get
When outsiders try to run their lives

Charlie was guarding the Defense Attaché
With an Eagle Scout from Iowa named Darwin Judge
At the Tan Son Nhut Airport outside Saigon
When a VC rocket targeting their shelter touched down

Poor brave Charlie
He was almost twenty-two
Less than two weeks gone in-country
One of the last two killed in action there
The next day the Americans were gone

Charlie's body had to be left behind
Grieving Charlie's mother, poor Mrs. McMahon
It took a full year until he could come home
To the leafy town he rode his bicycle in
Charlie paid the ultimate sacrifice
On the common they engraved his name
But how can the best and brightest be used,
Merely imperialist pawns in the game?

How can this game go on and on?
What is the sense in this plan?
For a nation to grow a Boy of the Year
If you waste the life of the man?

## Strip Mall in the Poconos

A breeze moves across the plateau
Carries damp essence of conifer in spring
Wisps of new life emerge in the country
Arrive among us late one Friday evening

Laconic strip mall, a concrete oasis
A highway rest stop for the urban evacuee
An excuse to escape the house for the restless teen
A minimum wage fallback producing low self-esteem

Empty parking lot is a launch pad for youth
A skateboard track, place for hacky sack
A catwalk to model Abercrombie and Fitch
Baggy jeans, washboard abs, exposed bra straps

A place to simply stand around and talk
Without their parents, teachers and cops
To laugh and brag and blow your top
And flirt with the one who you'd like to fuck

*Gossip Girl* or *The Hills*?
Kanye West or Fifty Cent?
Is *Grand Theft Auto* worth the money you spent?
Whose cell phone has the awesomest frills?

The clerks hang outside their empty shops
Smoking a butt to try to look cool
Eyeing the road to make out the headlights
Listening to the kids with an ironic grin

From my seat in the SUV
I cannot help but envy their youth
But I wouldn't go back, to tell you the truth
For the unasked questions that they have to face:

*How the hell do we get out of this mess?*
*Where do we go if we actually do?*
*How do we figure out what is real*
*And to let go of all that baggage which is less?*

## Poetry

Everywhere I go
It's poetry
Poetry
Is there for me
And if it's there for me
It's there for you
We are only
Different shades of blue

It's John Ford's Monument Valley
Or Miss O'Keefe's red clay plateaus
The *Giant Steps* taken by Coltrane
And Debussy's ringing glissandos

It's Yastrzemski in left
Clemente in right
It's MJ gliding into the paint
It's number 4, Bobby Orr,
Suspended in air
With the winning score

The Chrysler Building's silver flash
A lone figure in Tiananmen Square
The little Hispanic girl's smile
In the Chinese restaurant
That album cover's diamond raindrops
Sparkling Marvin Gaye's hair

And Christ in the desert
To me the sweetest poesy
In the heat of that vast moment
A cooling ointment deeply burning into me

Wherever you go
They say that's where you are
But poetry is what it does to you
Poetry is what you take away
Poetry is something to leave behind
When you reach your end of day.

## Elegy for a Fallen Poet

*(Ray Pospisil 1953-2008)*

Buttoned down anguish
Regular guy
Close shave maelstrom
Behind sunken eyes
Cool reserve pressed chinos
Faraway pallid smile
Wheels within wheels revealed
The workings of your inner mind
I remember you working it out
I remember you pacing the floor
On a sultry summer evening
In the muggy month of July
In the city of crashing subways
And smoky killer cars
Of insomniac static
And cold sweat staring dreams
You reasoned with the demons
Evaluating data streams
You had fun with the conundrum
Every breathing moment leaves:
Can we people live together?
Can mankind endure world pain?
Anxiety, destiny, guilt, grief,
Self-loathing and regret
The bulls and the bears and your federal reserve
Che Guevara and the baseball game
Snowfort sliding memories
With a hint of fresh rainbow shine.

I did not really know you
But could someone really know you?
I know it's hard to be a human being
A mighty challenge to be yourself
But I'll remember you pacing the floor
Rocking forward onto your toes
I wanted you to work it out
I wanted you to show me the way
But a poet is like a children's top
It topples when the momentum stops.

## Curious Poetry

The date on the calendar said October 6th
But the lemonade sun was blazing
Which made the Great Lawn juicily gleam
With healthy brilliance
And changed the hearts of men fresh green
That had turned as the autumn leaves.

Diamond number 3 was in high midsummer form
The red clay felt springy as muscle tone
Turning tourists' heads with
Transformative exuberance
As two dozen men over fifty
Played a game made for children

Receding grey hairlines and beer leaguer bellies
Decried the years and chide so cocksure
While proudly shirtless manboobs
Seemed to defy gravity
And geriatric kneebrace
Reinforces rusty heroes' wheels.

Friendly competition that drives them out for blood
Cigarettes at a jaunty angle
Throaty laughter with their gloves
Back-handed on jutting hips
Hoary mullets goad scruffy goatbeards
To hit rotating sphere.

Setting themselves:
Taut balance of their positions
Waiting on delivery of pitch
Waiting for one moment they can think of all off-season
Old man in lounge chair drolly watching
While he waits for certain death.

Let this be my curious brand of poetry
Not nice to look at but beautiful
Valuing friendship and endurance
Season in and out
Always ready for another game
In the Indian summer sun.

## Love Poem for an Australian Cyber-Fiancé

*(for WK)*

I'm rightside up
and
You're upside down
But I hang on your every word

You're so far away
You are beautiful
So I hope that my falling
Appears graceful online
That these words fill the cracks
Fracturing our faultlines
Weaves a thread that will lead
To the way we can't find
From "surfing the cusp"
To the ties that will bind

Always be mine
Let's never meet
Stay as you seem
Both tart and sweet

Always be there
Well out of reach
Kindly beware
Contact and speech

Absence makes the heart grow fonder
Opposites often attract
But distance brings us even closer
Sweet distance breeds other's jealousy
Distance a security blanket
Dang'rously enveloping me.

Peanut butter and jelly
Something called jatz and jam
Maybe I find it easier
You idealize who I am
When you push our virtual pram
Think of Bowie singing
"Total Blam Blam"
Makes me doff my bush hat
Howling, "G'Day, Ma'am!"

## Testament

I'm so full of feelings
Grasshopper green monkey bar feelings
Feelings that don't belong in respectable society
That are not 49 year old white male feelings

Feelings that make me vibrate inside in the dead of the night
That wish to break me open to hatch an escape
That want to dance around like a happy pinhead
That wonder how many happy pinheads can dance on the head of one pin

Feelings that cause people to give me curious looks
That piss people off for reasons they can't put their finger on
That would not be considered fiscally prudent
That don't leave any room for more practical things

I'm so full of feelings that have awesome mutant powers
That allow me to storm the battlements
That require me to prepare my acceptance speech
That are able to shit all the bullshit

Feelings that there aren't enough hours in the day for
Feelings that scat and declaim and Na na hey hey too
Feelings brought to you in living color sugar bubble pop
And bong water resin sticky icky laying back

I'm so full of feelings that won't let me off the hook
That sing the music of my Irish ancestors with a Boston accent
That somehow stumbled their Bowery way downtown
That now are part of the continuum

I'm so full of feelings that produce copious amounts of water from my eyes
That have been abandoned and betrayed by the one who had my faith
Feelings hopeless junkies and homeless poets have saved
That lay my head against the bark and let the spirits be praised

I'm so full of feelings that have no answers for the Big Questions
That long to turn and see the laughing face of Christ
That cry to God why did you take that one young man and in so doing
break my whole family
Feelings that have no way back from whence they came

I'm so full of feelings
Feelings that love

## Impossibility

Scent of juniper moves across the mountainside
Stirring naked branches fuzzy with buds
Crisscross angles checker sunshine and shadow
Gently dappling choking detritus
Pale reeds, sharp brambles and steaming compost
Yesterday's stubborn leftovers, a nest
Where the wild Hippogriff seeks cover

Tucked into himself, his wings a curtain
For his strange and fierce visage
He exhales deeply into his proud breast
As he listens to the twitter of birds flitting about him
The chirping of frogs emerging from deep sleep
Everything fresh and new and appealing
Everything but the myth itself

With foolish nobility and formal reserve
He frightened the curious away
He did not know if there was another like him
He was not sure if he was even real
But there was nothing to be done about that

He approached a young cow laying in the sweet grass
He felt certain that she was lonely
And did not care that she was not like him
He cantered for her delight
His hooves scattering clumps of sod
As he displayed his tawny plumage
But she did not know what to make of him
And shied away in fear

The Hippogriff let out an anguished cry
Which echoed down the mountainside
And beat his wings until he was aloft;
It was in flight that he revealed his beauty
Circling upward, catching the updraft

Climbing the expanse of sky; when he chose,
He could ascend with the swiftness of lightning,
Creating an amber streak in the heavens

The Hippogriff's tears rained down the mountainside
And buds broke into bloom
As quickly as a heart can break

Soon the Hippogriff had climbed so high
That even the great hawks looked up in wonder
From their soaring height
At the shrinking miracle overhead

The Hippogriff was hoping
He would disappear altogether;
But no matter how high he flew,
He could not escape himself.

## Spencer Tracy

Watching Spencer Tracy
On the silver screen:
Simple, principled
Softness to his strength
Fighting Irish gentility
A thoughtful calm
A surety
A playful ease
And never bumped into the furniture

But when the fleshy face creases
With his wry whiskey smile,
His eyes project the stations of the cross.

## New Year's Day

Jesus, those nails and thorns
And pierced side must have hurt
What a bloody way that was
To have to prove your point

And your disciples' denial
Was a kick in the pants
And when it seemed your Dad forsook you
Left you tacked up on a branch

But on New Year's Day, back in "0" A.D.
When you were only one week old
Your sufferings were well underway
When your cute little foreskin went and got moheled

Fumble bumble
A mohel can't stumble
One wrong flick of the wrist
Could leave our savior humbled

We need a circumcision
With an act of contrition
We wanna keep our conscience clean
While we maintain good down-low hygiene

It's true your body was divine
And you could turn water into wine
You could raise the dead and cure disease
But your willy was in danger of fromunda cheese

Fromunda cheese
Means, if you please
Cheese from unda
In your B.V.D.s

They say when they slice that mess away
A man loses sexual sensitivity
This is no big thing for a chaste deity
But a major setback for a horndog proclivity

I might've set off more hormones
With tree fungus, not a mushroom cap
You might as well make us feel more studly
If either way, we could end up with the clap

Snip, snip
There goes another tip
They toss them outside town, until
They build a mound they call Skull Hill

JC, I mean no disrespect,
'Cause after all, you conquered death
But with that li'l extra in your loincloth
The ladies may have to catch their breath

Instead, you teach a parable
About this very New Year's date
That every man will come up short
Practically out of the gate!

## Well, Come On!

The Stooges
Of Ann Arbor Michigan
Were finally being inducted
Into the Rock and Roll Hall of Fame
After being nominated seven times
Before and being passed up
By bands that they influenced:
The Ramones, Patti Smith Group.
The Sex Pistols. The Clash.

The naysayers said they were too primitive
They said they weren't good enough musicians
They said they didn't sell enough records
If there is going to be such a thing
As a Rock and Roll Hall of Fame
How can you deny the band
That set the template
For punk and hardcore
With the frontman
Who originated the stage dive
And took the art of antagonizing the audience
To a level even Jim Morrison didn't dream of

The former Jimmy Osterberg was thrashing
His tightly coiled body about the stage
As the band started up the intro
To *I Wanna Be Your Dog*
He looked up into the balcony
Where the few Stooges fans
Who could afford to come to the ceremony
Were dancing their asses off
And he flashed his still boyish smile
Then he looked down at the stageside tables
He bounded down into the audience
And began to deliver the song

To a table full of music industry suits
Iggy gave his all, yelping wildly
And punctuating the beat with pelvic thrusts
And these lawyers, who boogied ecstatically
When ABBA was inducted, sat stone-faced,
Arms folded tightly in front of them
Contemplating the creases in their trousers

While these parasites' industry is dying,
You can't kill the music
Iggy called the real fans up on stage with him
And at last, the losers won one!

## The Other Stooges

Shemp
Curly
Shemp again
Joe Besser
Curly Joe

You can come up with something
As a team
Make it your own                                    *(Shemp)*
Work at it
Take your lumps
While you strive to be noticed

Then when faced with unexpected abandonment
Let this be your moment of opportunity
When a familial act of faith
Produces singular genius
Untrained spontaneous invention
Causing brutally absurd joy:

"Little fly upon the wall                            *(Curly)*
 Ain't you got no clothes at all?
Ain't ya got no shimmy shirt?
Ain't ya got no petti-skirt?
Shoo fly!"

But genius burns bright
And tender hearts need
When all their running in circles
Prevents recognition
Of what everyone else can see
So your realization
Of this strange perfection
Flashes altogether briefly

Then fraternal loyalty
Must step in to save                                    *(Shemp again)*
All that you have worked for
And practiced professionalism
And shared effort
Enable the audience
To accept the transition
So at least you are better prepared
When a lighted match
Precedes a cigar exploding a stooge

Adapt to survive
Is the thing that is key
For a critically disrespected
Comedy team
For working stiffs who never
Got their fair due
Who know it all could be over
If they don't add up to three
One could never hit someone as hard
As you could hit your own brother
But when you run out of brothers,
You make do
And you work the bits and gags
With who the studio gives you                           *(Joe Besser)*
Until one day
The studio sends you home

But sometimes your accumulated effort
Brings you a curtain call
Though you may be more frail
And less inspired
The children appreciate
The way you made them smile                             *(Curly Joe)*

And they will embrace you
In whatever form you can present yourself
And it does not matter to you
For all you ever wanted
Was to go on working
Face slaps and foot stamps and skull cracks
And it is still working
Though you all are gone
The laughter goes on

Shemp
Curly
Shemp again
Joe Besser
Curly Joe

With
Larry
and
Moe.

# Easter Sunday

*(for Pär Lagerkvist & Christopher Frye)*

A layer of dust
Coated my garment bag
I guess I hadn't used it
Since the last funeral
I hoped that my mourning suit still fit
But there was nothing to be done about it

> Meanwhile, the criminal Barabbas
> Wonders, "What's the deal with these people?
> They never gave the slightest shit about me
> Or pissed their pants at the mention of my name
> They pleaded with the Romans to get me off the streets
> But now they spare my life over some preacher's?"

A travelling bag
Is such a grown-up thing
There are little compartments
For your underwear and socks
I count how many outfits I might need
A different shade of black each day of the week

> And the violent felon Barabbas
> Ponders, "What does it mean when you
> Murder the man who says LOVE, and you
> Let loose the one who cries out HATE?!
> For me, it makes me hate men more
> And sick to my stomach for poor foolish love"

My lone pair of dress shoes
Have seen more carefree days
But one thing they have not lost
Is their designer name
My feet will be blistered before I am done
You don't say a word when you have been struck dumb

Then the enslaved gladiator Barabbas
Boils within with conflict
His virtuous friend fights bravely in the ring
But the Romans strike him down when he won't finish
    the thing
Even though B. has heard the Word, the audience
    wants blood
So Anthony Quinn kills Jack Palance real good

My luggage on the train
To keep me company
I want my feet on the ground
I am in no hurry
To face the moving on that I feel I can't
Just a few more hours to try and understand

And lo, the unlikely martyr Barabbas
Suffers and dies on the cross
He fought alongside his Christian brothers
Though he never quite got their message
He just knew that the only thing worth believing in was love
And for his messy life, a way for him to make sense of.

## April is Gone

*(for JSE)*

Another lovely spring is running away;
Rushing through the spaces twixt my fingers as I grasp
Slipping like mercury fleet-footed through the sky
Dancing 'round the blossoms on the fly

How long, my dear, How long?
How long will you and I be a part of this song?
The spring will come as long as Time will go on
But we are like the blossoms:
We are here, and then we're gone.

## Tri-City Rock Brood

*(for Dalia Zatkin)*

We were there
In the downtown
Biker jacket black
Flat cardboard dance floor
Strasberg glamour
Spike heel, high-top
New York streets

While Buck Naked played
The rockabilly raw
In the city by the bay
And a cocaine flame
Blazed Texas blues
In the hands of Austin's
Stevie Ray

Yes, we were there
And we styled high hair
In the video jukebox
Smoky rock club
Safe sex spandex
Barrio helado
Cool as your idols
Schimmel's Knishes
Dope sick score kick
Freebase spray paint
New York dawn

When ol' Buck would be slain
Walking his dog by Golden Gate
By some nut who didn't want the pigeons chased
Cue *Teenage Pussy From Outer Space*
After Stevie Ray pitched his downward slide
Restarted clean, his skills applied
To play with kings until the sky cried
When his little wing kissed the mountainside

How life goes on
Like Donkey Kong
A sudden breeze comes up
To flip the pages of your *Rolling Stone*

Where are we
In a boutique Bowery
Starbucks Saint Mark's
IHOP Limelight
SoHo condo
Pedestrian walkway
Protected bike lane
Auto tuner
Bieber fever
New York now?

The voice on the BART train says,
"Please Hold On"

So
HOLD ON
There's a dive bar that smokes
Even though you can't light up
HOLD ON
Long as you've legs like that
We can dance our way
To bridge the gap
HOLD ON
The pigeons fly guilt-free,
The dogs give chase
Without a hint of blame
HOLD ON

Some kid on Youtube
Is copping every lick
Off Stevie Ray
HOLD ON
While Buck's guitar player
Was left forever bare-assed
Without his gig
HOLD ON
He bought me a beer
Because he learned I was
The band's newest fan!

HOLD ON
To the good
You got going
HOLD ON
To all the good
From before
Don't forget
That everything
Is its own reward.

## The Middle Ages

She takes pictures of herself
She posts on her online profile
From the camera in her cell phone
Extending it before her
As far as her arm can go
With the grace of her childhood ballet class
Carefully angling the shot
And the tousle of her hair
Or shooting herself straight on
In the bathroom mirror
Maybe she is waiting in the car
To pick up her kids
Or finally alone in the T.V. room
When everyone has gone to sleep

She is still beautiful
But she is working at something more
She is trying to capture
The best she ever looked
The lingering vitality
Of her carefree days
She may only want one man in the world
But she wants everyone to notice
That she is still here

## 25% Tip

It's so easy to fall in love
With the waitress
Especially when she gives you
Good service

Eating dinner alone again
I bring a book
To look less like a loser
My waitress a funky little pixie
Edie Sedgwick in Juicy Couture
Her smile of greeting leaves me
Instantly smitten
But she's got to be in her twenties
What a dirty old man I am!
Still she wants to know
The title that I'm reading
*Tales of Ordinary Madness*?
She likes that
'Cause madness really can be, like,
An everyday experience
So of course I agree
And I highly recommend it
Then she finds Bukowski's picture
Interesting
Well if that ugly old bastard is
Interesting
Then there's hope for all of us
Still
But after that,
It was hard to get a word with her
All those diners with their orders
And their refills and credit cards
Plus I didn't really know
What else to talk to her about
Next thing I know she's left

The check there on my table
And just when I think
The magic is over
I open it up and it's there
Inside

She's written, "Have a Great Night!"
And underlined the word "Great"
Thrice
And she's written her name,
Which is **Jackie**
But all around it were stars
Eight funny shaky stars
That's how she gave it to me:
My college girlfriend
Who wrote cryptic messages
On crazy torn bits of graph paper
The Polish graphic artist
Who glued little figures
On a painted card
My missing wife
Penned an abstract runic garden
Around her message
A constellation of expression
That stirred the scarlet ink
Filling my heart

It's so easy to fall in love
With the waitress
Especially when she gives you
Good service.

## Buk Drops In

I was sitting on the toilet
In my dirty apartment
I was wiping my ass with my left hand
As the Prophet decrees
And smoking a cigar with my right
And this made me think of Bukowski
And there he was!
Laying on the cold tile floor
Waiting for his chance to puke

"What the fuck are you looking at?!"
He barked
"You have no right to judge me.
You don't work hard enough.
You don't get drunk enough.
You write too many goddamn rhyming poems!"

I told him I didn't mean to stare
But it was amazing to see him again.

"You ain't shittin' it's amazing,"
Buk burped
"Just try and get T.S. Eliot or Robert Frost
To appear on demand. Fat chance!"

He snatched my stogie from me

"We miss you, Buk,"
I said
"There's nobody else like you
To show us how to go on."

"Aw, Christ!"
Hank spat
"You whine like such a woman,
I expected there to be cute lace panties
Twisted around your ankles there."

His head was ringed with cigar smoke

"Same things that could bring me back
From the beyond is what keeps you going.
Booze, pussy and a little music on the radio."
He flicked the cigar butt at my feet

"Now can you get off the crapper
And give somebody else a chance?!"

## John Sinclair

In Tompkins Square Park
They were having a rally
For the Million Marijuana March

The stoners were out en masse
To hear some wild-eyed shaman
Disseminate drug policy

While there were groups
Of twitchy cops
On all sides

So every once and awhile
Some yahoo would light one up
Then the cops would pounce
And drag them away

In the middle of it all
Sinclair sat on a bench
Taking long draws off a
Perfectly rolled joint
Watching everything
With an ironic grin

He's seen it all and
Lived to shake his head
And roll his eyes
At the elusive passage of time:
The more things change
The more they are frozen in place

And I know better not
To ask him for a hit
Because I am not similarly
Camouflaged with wisdom

So instead I thought of
A joint I smoked with him
Outside a jazz club in Brooklyn
With Sun Ra's alto sax wailer
The ginger red siren screaming
Marshall Allen:
In the cool snap shirt sleeve evening
Wily eyes exchanged flashing inspiration
Through cataract film and drooping lids
Knowing smiles spread spider lines
As they piled one story on top of another
Like a hard bop house of cards
John at 70 and Marshall at 80
Giggling together like children
While a rattle in their chests
Acts as an echo to remind us
To mark their example while we can:

      Ingrain yourself in the culture
      To live what you love

      Do what you can do

        Don't mind the bastards

          Bide your time

            Agitate from within

              And have a fucking great time
              Doing it.

## Sharp Blue Stream

*(for William Hawkins and Alan Moore)*

Here I am in the blue
Submerged in this hue
For so long
It's hard to say, "So long"

Candy apple red
And bullshit brown
Mixed a murk so deep
That I almost drowned

Now I'm buoyed by cobalt
Yardbird cadenza stream flow
Hand painted silent frame chill
Ecstatic palette of van Gogh

But I think of mighty Doctor Manhattan
Covered cerulean head to toe
Contemplative on a barren planet
Of the lovely moments he's ceased to know:

A woman slowly brushing her hair
The mirror image in which she stares
Scent of perfume he bought hangs in air
Simple miracle of her lounging in her underwear

Then this aquamarine brilliantine
Adherence to the crime of the scene
The part of me that wishes I were dead
Must be shorn away, sunk in chains of lead

Way down to the bottom-most depths
A place where the sun does not shine
So the blue there is so dark that it's black
Then these ties will no longer bind

I skim along cornflower skin like a stone
Hatch a robin's egg flight toward auroral dawn
Leave my sapphire music hung in the air
Because I must be moving on.

## Yorkville

These streets we strolled on
Worked ourselves out on
That the dog walked us on

The streets where Walter Kucker,
The last angry German Towner,
Causes college kids to cross
To the other side of the block
With his pit bulls at his side
And his own Rottweiler face

Where once the Bavarian Dorothy Jahn
Showed off her legs
Dancing the waltz
At the Gloria Palast
Burning enough calories
For a strudel afterwards
At the Kleine Konditorei

Where Mrs. Hilska from apartment 3C
Demonstrated her Czech spirit
And physical flexibility
In daily gymnastic classes
At the Sokol Hall
Down on 71st Street

Where Teamsters who were still called
Krauts by their Mick union brothers
At the Jacob Ruppert Brewery
Took their frustrations out on
The German American Bund
Hitting them over the head
With their own pro-Fascist placards

Where the young Marx Brothers
Ran wild in the east nineties
Cutting up and cutting school
Where the cocky little Cagney kid
Gave his alibi in perfect Yiddish
To confound the apple polisher on the beat

Where the Cooz first dribbled a basketball
Where the Iron Horse took his first cuts

We were making our own history
And you left me with the gentrification
The Ideal Restaurant and the Yorkville Inn are gone
And for this we get a cavernous Barnes and Noble
Filled with yuppie bitches with jogging strollers
Containing the bankers of the future
Who will finally price me out.

## Space

In the space down below
Behind the curtains
A place where you don't think to look
To such an extent that

Years can go by

And you have no idea what is there

So years do go by

And I don't know what there is
Which has lost the meaning it once had
Because of the fuck I did not give to care
Its existence has receded into the dim region of
negligence

But things fall apart
As we already know
And corners can crumble
Like dry breakfast cereal

When the goblins on the other side of things
Flex their muscles of hot breath
And that green color of past generations
Spews forth like the vomit of ghosts

Bringing me face to face
With the shrouded wraith of compromise
The one-eyed blinking frog in a suit of clankering tin
Gasping his emptiness of abandonment

And I still had to bite down
On my sympathy
Crush the heart of my
Nostalgia for random history

And threw my hands wide
As I displaced its constancy
For perhaps it is now

Finally now

That I have opened the space
Through which a soft and slender fingertip
May reach through.

## String Arrangement by Van Dyke Parks

Something huge
Is pushing against
A steady wind
Starboard bound
Toward open sea
Perilous
Epic in its simplicity
You can feel it inside
Where everything is wet
And sometimes seeps out
So you must swab the deck
Exquisite tension swells
Excruciating regret
My guts are quivering
In that way you can't help
As little white capped peaks
Blanket toss me heavenward
Joyful gulps of release
From the vast incomprehensible

Van Dyke Parks nods,
Pencil in hand
At his solitary scoring table
He is the copyist
Of the transcendent
He has witnessed
The mundane transformed
By five part harmony
Making figures in motion
Fragment and blur
Into the realm
Of the abstract
Riding a crest
Of diamond sunshine
With such stillness,
That it seemed effortless

But something so precious
Can easily crack
And never be the same again
And you and I
And Van Dyke Parks
Brushing away pencil shavings
At his scoring table
Wish that it wasn't so

But the diminuendo
Pulls the twilight down
Like a horse blanket
Spread on a sandy shore
And on the smudge pot driftwood
Hemp smoke breeze
A mournful accordion is heard
Performing sea shanties.

## TV Screen Reflection

Shit kicker getaway car
On an episode of *Cops*
Running from domestic disturbance
No one on the roadway understands

It's lost one of its tires
And it's riding on the rim
And the sparks are flying up
Just like the Fourth of July

Skipping into the breakdown lane
Like a thousand beflicked Pall Mall butts
Reanimating burnt rubber skid marks
Causing state policeman's reverie 'bout
Sleep-away camp lightning bugs

Speakers jamming *Radar Love*
White lines flying past
Evening air so fresh and cool
The sirens sound like victory

And no one sees the sense of running
When you're bleeding precious fluids out most constantly
And with the roadblocks up ahead, it's pathetic
But see the convoy in your rearview, and you have to laugh

For everything, you reach a point in existence
When you know despite of all that you cannot stop
Or there is simply no start up again
Then you hear the auto graveyard's rusty call:

*"Sad boys, sad boys*
*Whatcha gonna do?*
*Whatcha gonna do*
*When nothing's left to you?"*

## Suburbia Redux

Gasoline vapors trail
An unseen lawn mower's motor
On a day awash in sunshine
I remember ever new

Lazy ballgame radio
Narrates our wait for sudden action
Dimly fading cartoon playroom
Illuminates the buzzing day

Bumblebees and bicycles
Motor oil spots and dog's wet noses
Line drying laundry and dragonfly wings

You could wander anywhere on this day
It didn't mean anything that you were alone
You could do anything on this day
That's why you'd end up doing nothing at all.

## Between a Brother and Sister

One time
I got my
Big toe stomped
Playing ball
And the nail
Turned black and
Fell off;
So I put it
In an envelope
And sent it
In the mail
To my sister

And then
My sister
Had some girl
From China
Shave callous
Off her foot
And she mailed
That to me

So you can see
By all of this
That we were
Very close.

## Zouk

Out of the pitch dark nightlife of Brooklyn
Feet stumbling for a dance step
Salsa rhythms thrust upon me
Lone star pulsing overhead
Flood of stars filling my eyes
Black sedan rolls down slow
Sure of fares, full of gas
Fearing no child of man
It opens its hatch wide
And swallows us, holy

Behind the wheel an island man
Bizarro Caribbean Charon
Coolly guiding us safely homeward
To a livelier state of mind
His radio pumping out joy juice
Bubble beat machine Creole serenity
Fruity groove parade carnival booty skoot
Those who are brightly feathered understand

Oh, don't touch that station, my brother
I've an inkling your soundtrack can help me
I had a problem with making adjustments
But can lay my head back in here really fine
Light streaks speed alongside our journey
Hot molten gold spewed to mark our trajectory
Ecstatic tracers of forms when in motion
Industrial scenes are a glow smear abstraction

I don't know
You don't know
They don't know too
It doesn't matter much anyway
Everything just may well be everything
But some things are better still just the same

That belly dancer and her creamy undulations
The filthy courtship between the cock and the hen
You may never really know how sad I was
Look in the window now and you will see me smiling
These secretarial pool shoulder shimmyers
Those weekend warriors armed with conga drums
I don't know where all these people are headed
But I pray that it is where they want to go

I don't know if I can ever change myself
But maybe I can change up everything else
So many things I've seen have never come to pass
Perhaps this wondrous vision shows me what is always
I stretch my hands up toward the sky
And I am dancing with my sister
Then my father grabs her arm and jumps around
And in the homeland of my ancestors,

A cloud of sod gets kicked up from the ground.

## Chanticleer

Rooster in the graveyard
At the crick neck crack of dawn
This stern burgeoning necropolis
With snooze button on hold

Rooster in the graveyard
Bantam game cock of the walk
Once we stretched our bodies on your dust
And hoped you'd cop a feel

Yawning crypts and grey sepulchres
Little plates set in the ground
Free of carrion columbarium
Cairn close to where the blackthorn grows

Dorothy can see Celia's house from here
Teeth marks on a piece of chewing gum
That hot shit Bobby Kane used his brain
To split a Bedford Road telephone pole

Knock knock, who's there?
Jackie Gleason's under where
Has left the building for Graceland
Or Wacko Jacko's Neverland

That bell's the deadbeat ice cream man
Fred MacMurray in a little box
A shaky bakey song on baritone horn
While libations are poured on the polishing stone

My legacy's under holy hood
Where stony bony fingers coax
A Corman era Vincent Price with
Red and white wax candy fangs

A silent shroud by Mister Graves
An island unto Dan himself
Six sacred scarabs scuttle from
A wise owl dining on a vole

Rooster in the graveyard
Puffed up pleased and proud as Punch
The worms crawl in to eat some crow
Trav'ling over landscape architects

Rooster in the graveyard
That Simon Peter can't deny
Bounce your clarion off that rock cut tomb
Trump card Lazarus from the tumuli

Take my hand as if I was a child
Shake every rattle that you've got
I'll bring a droll soul parade with me
Across the bridge from which she can't get back

To Gertrude poised on her unibike
Her thoughtful copper penny outfit shines
A smile for to tell me it's alright
A swarm of birdsong just before the fall of night.

## The 31st of May

Gaping morning rear window
Aspires expansive air freshness
Shotguns breath of new life
Into my morbid old worldview
High definition bedazzlement
Deep focus green shades shine
My tired eyes now energized
By wildflower's electric fluorescence
Newness grows on top of oldness
Vibrant voices call across the expanse
Shimmering trees bend back
Against the wind
Like Maureen O'Hara might throw
Her head back on the strand
Sending glistening tracers of color
Alongside a sapphire canvas of sky

Oh, dread personification of Death
Why the hell don't you go fuck yourself?
You can't be everywhere at once
And the minute your dark back is turned
The day hangs momentary jewels
On a stand of little purple flowers
And there's nothing you can do about it.

## Mokombwe

There is a stream
That runs through everything
Vital, primal
Well-spring
Moving deep beneath the surface of all
Drawing down thirsty roots
Rising up to quench us
Rushing forth to make music
Against smooth stones
A positive current beneath your feet

There is a stream
That flows through my body
Complex, basic
Plasma
Nourishing breath and reflex
Fueling inspiration and action
Conducting electrical impulse
Which fires five senses
A momentary harness for eternal spirit

The tinkling of the sewers
On Fowle Street in Woburn
When I was seventeen
Was trying to tell me something
A shipwrecked man
Clinging to a spar
Sometimes only need relax
And turn onto his back

There is a stream
That runs through Time itself
Eternal, familial
Rocket's tail
Guiding you backwards and forwards
Whispering secret knowledge
Teaching you the steps to
Dance your cares away
An astral trail blazed by the first ancestor

Let go.

DAVID LAWTON is a native of Woburn, Massachusetts, and a graduate of the Theatre Performance program at Boston University, where he was also a Guest Artist in the Graduate Playwriting classes taught by Nobel Laureate (in poetry) Derek Walcott. He has acted in several Off-Broadway plays, and had his plays performed Off-Off Broadway. For 10 years, he sang background vocals with the late 80s underground band Leisure Class. At the band's de facto headquarters in the Chelsea Hotel, he befriended Beat godfather Herbert Huncke and San Francisco poet Marty Matz and was inspired by their embodiment of the written word.

### *Acknowledgements*

My gratitude must go out first to Peter Carlaftes and Kat Georges, who took on this project and saw it through to the end, so that I might thank the following people: To my mother, Betty Lawton, who teaches me every day how to keep moving. To all the teachers who helped prepare me, and three: Herbert Huncke, Marty Matz and John Sinclair, who showed me (and in John's case, who still does) how to live the life. To all the gifted and unique people I have met in the New York City poetry community who are too numerous to mention, and especially my friends Thomas Fucaloro, Jane Ormerod, Puma Perl, George Wallace, and Obsidian and Hobo Bob. And to my friends Paul Romero, Dan Gately, Dimitri Mobengo Mugianis, my brother Paul Lawton, Julie Eakin, Mary Walsh, Maya Rath, Dan Carew, Kevin Coughlan, Dan Porvin, Melissa Schaffer, Elizabeth Morales, Christine & Jenny Westberg, Kombi & Bovenga, who all helped get me through a painful time in my life so that it could produce poetry.

# books on three rooms press

## POETRY

Hala Alyan
*Atrium*

Peter Carlaftes
*DrunkYard Dog*
*I Fold with the Hand I Was Dealt*

Joie Cook
*When Night Salutes the Dawn*

Thomas Fucaloro
*Inheriting Craziness is Like*
*  a Soft Halo of Light*

Patrizia Gattaceca
*Isula d'Anima / Soul Island*

Kat Georges
*Our Lady of the Hunger*
*Punk Rock Journal*

Robert Gibbons
*Close to the Tree*

Karen Hildebrand
*One Foot Out the Door*
*Take a Shot at Love*

Matthew Hupert
*Ism is a Retrovirus*

David Lawton
*Sharp Blue Stream*

Jane LeCroy
*Signature Play*

Dominique Lowell
*Sit Yr Ass Down or You Ain't gettin*
*  no Burger King*

Jane Ormerod
*Recreational Vehicles on Fire*
*Welcome to the Museum of Cattle*

Jackie Sheeler
*to[o] long*

Angelo Verga
*Praise for What Remains*

George Wallace
*Poppin' Johnny*
*EOS: Abductor of Men*

## PHOTOGRAPHY-MEMOIR

Mike Watt
*On & Off Bass*

## FICTION

Michael T. Fournier
*Hidden Wheel*

Richard Vetere
*The Writers Afterlife*

## DADA

*Maintenant: Journal of*
*Contemporary Dada Art & Literature*
(Annual poetry/art journal, since 2003)

## SHORT STORIES

*Have a NYC: New York Short Stories*
Annual Short Fiction Anthology

## HUMOR

Peter Carlaftes
*A Year on Facebook*

## PLAYS

Madeline Artenberg &
Karen Hildebrand
*The Old In-and-Out*

Peter Carlaftes
*Triumph For Rent (3 Plays)*
*Teatrophy (3 More Plays)*

Larry Myers
*Mary Anderson's Encore*
*Twitter Theater*

## TRANSLATIONS

Patrizia Gattaceca
*Isula d'Anima / Soul Island*
(poems in Corsican with
English translations)

George Wallace
*EOS: Abductor of Men* (American poems
with Greek translations)

**three rooms press**  | new york, ny
current catalog: www.threeroomspress.com